More Revolutionary Letters

a tribute to Diane di Prima

a Wisdom Body Publication

We have the right to make the universe we dream.

                Revolutionary Letter #51

we begin the work
may it continue
the great transmutation
may it continue

                Revolutionary Letter #68

                –Diane di Prima

ISBN: 978-1-7369770-0-2
Copyright © Wisdom Body Collective 2021

Table of Contents

MA REVOLUTION . . . 7
HALLOWEEN BLUE MOON . . . 13
Ode to the Kingfisher . . . 14
revolutionary letter in the shape of honey . . . 15
Revolutionary Letters 1-36: An Anarchic Cento . . . 16
THE ALJUBE, FOR INSTANCE . . . 18
Revolutionary Letter Proclamation . . . 20
In the language of night revolution . . . 23
Revolutionary Letter 2021 . . . 24
Revolutionary Letter # . . . 26
Revolutionary Letter: Decreation . . . 28
Revolutionary Letter: This Never Before Owned Red . . . 29
I Am Alive . . . 32
I Who Am Neither . . . 34
it'a come (for Diane di Prima) . . . 36
Revolutionary Letter 2021 . . . 38
My black-haired Cherokee Indian Princess . . . 39
Revolutionary Letter . . . 42
Rasp of the Revolutionary . . . 46
Revolutionary Letter #1 [B] . . . 48
*** . . . 50
Living but Dead Humans . . . 54
Religion Hiding in The Bush . . . 55
I ask myself the questions to walk the labyrinth city... . . . 58
Revolutionary Letter: Small Stirrings . . . 60
Revolutionary Letter: Dianesque . . . 62
Old Sedan (Revolutionary Letter 2020) . . . 64
Revolutionary Letter for Pear Tree . . . 66
WEFT 3 . . . 68
Revolutionary Letter . . . 70
Dear Kin, . . . 72
October 26, 2020 . . . 74
i do not believe in death . . . 76

MA REVOLUTION
an introduction to More Revolutionary Letters

Berkeley once held a great many collectives and co-ops, non-Capitalist worker-run outfits that bloomed in the late sixties. For a couple of years I worked at Bookpeople, a distributor of books that mainstream outlets avoided. The major items we shipped were Gay and Lesbian literature, grow your own dope books, a fix your VW handbook, and a thousand of the best poetry titles available. I worked receiving pallets of books, packing up orders for visionary bookshops, driving the delivery truck; and I learnt the nuances of just about every quality bookstore, from San Francisco's City Lights to Toronto's Lavender Menace.

At Bookpeople we also published a few titles, under the imprint Wingbow Press. The holiest of these were Diane di Prima's *Loba* and Edward Dorn's *Gunslinger*. Both are iconic poems; don't let that overshadow the steel-eyed revolutionary verse they hold. Diane's book-cover crimson, Ed's was bone white: like datura flowers of poetry-in-exile. Among the important volumes we posted to bookshops across the nation was a City Lights title, *Revolutionary Letters*. Its Lawrence Ferlinghetti cover was designed to make the Capitalist world falter: big rough-scrawled letters, rebellious red on black, like a poster blown in from Cuba.

```
R E V O
L U T I O
N A R Y
L E T T E R S
DIANE DI PRIMA
```

Who wouldn't pick that up for a few dollars? It came out in 1971, getting updated in 1974 with fifteen more poems, and kept growing for fifty years until Diane's death this past October.

Back in 1971, the year *Revolutionary Letters* came into print, Telegraph Avenue had a funny co-op warren of shops called The Old Garage, originally an auto repair place. By the late sixties the auto repair had gone and the space reopened with cheap rent. An undecorated large room selling food was called Ma Revolution's. The place looked like a repair shop. Concrete floor, industrial brick, salvaged wood. Except instead of old auto parts, wooden barrels of rice, bins of lentils, wheat, nuts, dry fruit; and packing crates with leafy vegetables. I heard it was the original natural food store in the country. It had none of the fancy over-hyped fare you get in groceries today. This was a time "revolution was in the air," a revolution not separate from ecological clarity, food that wouldn't poison you, and children who ran about in hand-me-down clothes. Diane di Prima's *Letters* were everywhere. She read them at cafes and rock shows, they were tacked up on walls and telephone poles, they appeared in the *Berkeley Barb,* and in anti-war anthologies.

The letters put blood in the eyes of young readers. They were motherly, fierce, sexy, cautionary, unflinching. Diane di Prima was the real deal, the authentic Ma Revolution. She'd raised children and knew what the young needed. "Our babes toddle barefoot through the streets of the Universe." She'd led an earlier life in New York, writing poems and editing the fleet 1960s pamphlet *Floating Bear* with LeRoi Jones. LeRoi soon went over to the Nation of Islam and changed his name to Amiri Baraka. About the same time, 1967 or -8, Diane headed West to San Francisco to work with the Diggers. The Diggers were a theater troupe committed to feeding hungry people, unmasking the war makers, making tribal life & eco concerns seem the most fun you could have. They performed unpredictable street theater, and whisked poetry out overnight, which writers and printers tossed from the beds of pickup trucks at dawn. We will never know how many bold, brave, compassionate acts Diane's revolutionary letters provoked. She wrote them for dharma revolutionaries. They speak to the moment not to the English Department.

If I slam my fist on the table I still won't convey how much spiritual authority Diane held in San Francisco. She was feeding a tribe & spoke of revolution like she'd been there. She studied Buddhism with Shunryu Suzuki; she read books in Sanskrit. She was plotting wise eco-policy with Gary Snyder, helping him build the manifesto "Four Changes." She wrote, gave readings, taught magic, knew herbs, studied hermetic lore. Counterculture printers issued her books. That in itself was a big gesture. Non-commercial publishing was the mode of the revolution.

I was walking on Guerrero Street, 1990, with my wife and two year old kid, heading to a friend's loft for a poetry salon. The night was foggy and cold. Althea, excited to be out late, ran a circle around a woman also going to the salon; it was Diane. She looked at the little girl dancing—turquoise tights and a purple quilted vest—under the streetlight. "That looks like an East Bay child," she said with such bemused authority that Althea turned and gave her a fizzly smile. Ma Revolution indeed.

I find it hard to imagine, but Diane had been a newcomer to the great city once. She told me that Moe Moskowitz (who everyone knew ran the best bookstore in the country, and who had been my boss for eight years), appeared as a one man welcome-committee when she'd shown up in the Bay Area. Moe knew her from anarchist circles back in New York, meetings and anti-war protests. I wonder if he knew Diane's grandfather, who she invokes in the opening poem of *Letters*. However far back their friendship stretched, "Moe let me know from the start that I was part of the tribe," she said in Berkeley, after Moe died in 1997.

About that same year, visiting the Jack Kerouac School, Diane told the assembled writers: You can get last generation's printing equipment for nearly nothing. Sometimes just for carrying it off. But watch out the previous "generation" machines—they've gotten boutique and cost a lot of money.

She pointed towards Naropa's Harry Smith Print Shop: "You bought that gear just in time." I saw this was her approach to revolution too; stay out ahead or the establishment will nullify you with dollars. Didn't she tell us, "Mao was fifty / years ago, and in China"? It's remarkable to note that her first *Revolutionary Letters* were "fifty years ago, and in San Francisco."

What keeps Diane's letters fresh is the hard good sense. Plenty of merry elves assume revolution comes easy. Healthy food, good sex, dancing, a few poetry readings. Diane saw how this makes activists vulnerable. Rough police tactics, reactionary lies, buy-outs for poets, need a smarter response. Her "letters"—notice the intimacy of the title—carry seasoned, practical counsel. They are directed to you. Diane knew Amiri had been beaten by the Newark cops. The city had arraigned him on weapons charges and resisting arrest. (Baraka says that in court the DA would read from his poetry, to show how dangerous he was, putting in "blankety-blank" for certain words. Amiri would turn to the Judge, "Your Honor, for the record, the word is motherfucker.") Diane had no illusions how cruel the response to revolution might be. Even though revolution could be simple & intimate, just living by rules of your tribe, procuring safe food, raising your children, making underground books.

In "Letter #3" she gives an ideogram of police tactics: "they turned off the water / in the 4th ward for a whole day during the Newark riots." Yes, they might turn off your water. For a mother this was serious. Keep your bathtub full of fresh water. This is what made Diane special. Her revolution was not for isolationists. It was for friends, lovers, parents and babies. She gave sound advice: "dry stuff like rice and beans stores best"—which was what Berkeley's Ma Revolution sold; "dried fruits and nuts / add nutrients." In "Letter #18" the stakes get higher: in your VW bus, stockpile "food, water, matches, clothing, blankets, gas." And as a rebuke to the Stalinists, she puts in caps, "NO ONE WAY WORKS." To move lightly, and to improvise, seem to be what work. Even if things keep getting tough, and revolution looks like a goal that keeps receding into the distance.

So fifty years later, what ways might work? You can begin by reading the transcript of her "Inaugural Address," when she got appointed Poet Laureate of San Francisco. In it she cautions against "the UnPhun Party," and releases a powerful vow to remind everyone that there is no season that is not "a Season of Song."

Here, then, as we enter another season of song, is a fistful of *More Revolutionary Letters.* Many by writers not even born when Diane began her letters. This volume is not so much a tribute as an effort to continue the work Diane di Prima began. Poets at The Jack Kerouac School have compiled it. The Kerouac School: a place Diane helped inaugurate, from the ground up, in 1974.

One day I'd like to talk about Diane's studies in Sanskrit, her wildly gorgeous journals, her studied lectures on poets H.D. and Ezra Pound. But today when I think of her late difficult years, her need for money for dental work, operations on her worn-out back, and how much she gave younger poets, I feel reverential and angry. How about instead of silly grants (a few bucks for a poet so the moneymakers can attach their own names)—how about real provisions? Like health care for life. Like guaranteed food, or college for children? See what you can envision, Reader. Take a careful look at these *More Revolutionary Letters.* Pray they provoke some magic or mischief, and a glimpse into revolutions of the future.

–Andrew Schelling
February 2021

HALLOWEEN BLUE MOON
a revolutionary letter

A singular, new version of
Jaime's werewolf poem showed up
in the mailbox tonight
the moon rose bloody cold over Kansas.
Sunday came death news Diane di Prima
author'd American she-wolf
epic *Loba*.
On Thursday Sect. of the Interior
doughy white David Bernhardt,
illicitly appointed
plus no credentials whatever,
delisted American gray wolf from endangered
status. Fat hands, the hunting lobby
feeds him. (Tonight Farmer's Almanac lists
full Hunter's Moon no shit—
Gray wolf protected 1973
keystone to the Endangered Species Act
forty-seven years ago,
same year first *Loba* poems
show up copyright fugitive small presses
Who else remembers Bardo Matrix?
    ((wolf howl mourn here, sign
Diane wolf paw print
end needless killing critters forever.

– Andrew Schelling
2020

Andrew Schelling is a poet, translator, and land use activist. Teaches poetry at the Jack Kerouac School, and Sanskrit for Naropa University's Buddhism and Yoga studies.

Recent books: *The Facts at Dog Tank Spring* (poetry) and *Songs of the Sons and Daughters of Buddha*, translations with Anne Waldman of early Indian wandering mendicants.

Ode to the Kingfisher

Dear god of wind, dear morning star—

> give me a glimpse of your cobalt crown, your persimmon throat. Pluck me from my mudbank and carry me home in your mouth, dislodge my bones and fashion them into flutes. Cling to me like the earth clings to your tangled roots, tunnel me through termitaria each evening, and swallow me like soft wood so I can live inside your chest, if only briefly. I will unhinge for you like a water-weakened shell. I will rid myself of running like the hunted hare pinned to an open field. Only then will I know each stone unturned, each seed unearthed.

> Only then will I be able to fly.

– Sarah Alcaide-Escue

---

*First published in *Channel Magazine*.

I always read *Revolutionary Letters* as a love letter to the world. Diane di Prima's work has given me permission to sit with my grief and rage, as well as my desire and joy. Ultimately, she's taught me to live and love unapologetically.

Sarah Alcaide-Escue is a writer and artist from Florida. She is the author of *Bruised Gospel* (The Lune, 2020), and she earned her MFA in Creative Writing and Poetics from Naropa University. Her work has appeared in *Mud Season Review, The Literary Review, The Meadow, *apo- press, Always Crashing,* and elsewhere.

revolutionary letter in the shape of honey

*"let no one work for another
except for love"*

i spit the names of my friends
into glimmering oysters and
splinter the neck of love;
four of us, sharing a bed,
our pearlescent feet
barely touching—
it is a closeness that would make
even orchids blush.
the scripture of our hollowed-out
night charts full bellies and
the veil of warmth;
so nascent, this enclave,
the entropy of our desire.
is this not a revolution?
yes, the corridor of shared meals,
of illuminated heads, must be
*and how would you like to
be received?*
gently, i say,
and with much conviction.

– Chloe Tsolakoglou

Chloe Tsolakoglou is a Greek-American writer who grew up in Athens, Greece. She is a graduate of the Jack Kerouac School, where she served as the Anselm Hollo Fellow. Her work oscillates between light and the clearing.

Revolutionary Letters 1-36: An Anarchic Cento

so that the stars can look down on the earth and not
be ashamed of us

the stakes are ourselves
get up
make a habit
plant seeds
you may be called upon
to practice
at any time, to die
it will take all of us

& no one 'owns' the land
this continent is seed
(across fields of insecticide and migrant workers)
subtle hieroglyphs of oracle
put back the buffalo

are you prepared
to do it
for our children's children, we will have to
will have to give up something
it's a good idea

you can have what you ask for, ask for everything
no black cloud fear or guilt
can you
do you care
to be spectator, on this scene where there are no spectators
have you thought about the American aborigines
whom you can summon in your neighborhood
'DOES THE END JUSTIFY THE MEANS?'
how much can we afford to lose, before we win

while the sun goes down on this fabled & holy land
no exile where we will not hear welcome home
remember they buyout all the leaders
better we should all have homemade flutes

simply the acts of song
the more we give up the more we will be blessed
put metal back in the earth, or at least not take it out anymore
the peace we seek was never seen before
stand clear

– Lisa Alvarez

Lisa Alvarez's poetry has appeared in *Borderlands: Texas Poetry Review*, *Huizache*, *TAB Journal* and most recently in *So It Goes*, the literary journal of the Kurt Vonnegut Museum and Library. She grew up in and around Los Angeles but has spent the last 30 years in Orange County, California where she earned an MFA in fiction from UC Irvine, and became a professor at the local community college. During the summers, she co-directs the Writers Workshops at the Community of Writers in the California's Sierra Nevada.

THE ALJUBE, FOR INSTANCE

nenhum fascismo w/out
violation of physical
integrity for instance
statue torture THE SWELLING
OF THE FEET & LEGS & THE
WEIGHT OF THE HEAD AS
IF IT WERE ABOUT TO
EXPLODE   WHEN THE
                              PRISONER LET HIMSELF
                              FALL HE RECEIVED KICKS
                              IN ALL PARTS OF THE
                              BODY
the PENS or DRAWERS 14
small cells located on
the 2nd floor   MADE TO FIT A
                              MAN LYING DOWN

a polícia politica foi a
principal executora desses
crimes, instrumento
primeiro da politica
da ditadura e dos
                              seus chefes

    the political police   ALWAYS USED
                              BEATINGS, FOLLOWING
                              PRECISE INSTRUCTIONS
                              FROM THEIR SUPERIORS
                              & GENERALLY USING
                              CUDGELS & BATONS
muscle aches joint
pain fractures sprains dis-
locations urinary in-
continence rectal lesions
back pain headaches panic
attacks locomotion problems
swollen legs swollen
                        feet

>   PREPARE YOURSELF YOU'RE
>   GOING TO THE MACHINE I
>   SAT DOWN THEY PUT A
>   HELMET ON MY HEAD SWITCHED
>   SOME LIGHTS ON I STARTED
>   TO FEEL SOME SHOCKS THAT
>   WERE NATURALLY ELECTRIC
>   SHOCKS

(música da resistência / protest song)

>   A. GENERAL REMARKS
>   B. THE STRUCTURE OF THE
>   INTERROGATION
>
>   1. THE OPENING
>   2. THE RECONNAISSANCE
>   3. THE DETAILED QUESTIONING
>   4. THE CONCLUSION
>
>   THE THEORY OF COERCION ARREST
>   DETENTION DEPRIVATION OF
>   SENSORY STIMULI THREATS &
>   FEAR DEBILITY PAIN

at the start of the
1970s in the barracks
of the colonial war the
young men were listening
to zéca afonso & adriano
correia de oliveira the
regime

>   CONTROLLED THEIR BODIES

> *– Max Henninger*

Max Henninger is a writer and translator based in Berlin. He has published in *Datableed, Tiny Spoon, Streetcake* and elsewhere. He was introduced to the poetry of Diane di Prima by the late Sean Bonney.

Revolutionary Letter Proclamation

This is the Antithesis Reality

"When the mode of the music changes, the walls of the city shake"

for Diane di Prima, in memoriam

We're coming out of our little theatres
Of hope & fear
To a city near you
We'll breathe again on the streets
& liberate the hall of justice and
We are the antithesis reality
All is brought to transparency
Twilight cannot be delayed
This is the antithesis reality
It's a deluge of fire
Of climate apocalypse
Watching the bloody moons & magenta suns
of dust & smoke dynamite the sky
Roiling in polite society
In a "gentleman's agreement"
In the sick corridors of corruption
Where *the fix is in, the fix is in*
And nano-racism & "hydraulic racism"
Haunt the premises
But this is the antithesis reality coming at you
Can't pull the wool over antithesis reality's eyes

The security state thrives on insecurity
And a war on daily life itself
Call in the paramilitaries, summon the Space Force
Put A TOKEN WOMAN ON THE MOON?

We're taking down oligarchy's assault!
Antithesis reality against psychopathic data flows
Damming up rabbit holes of disinformation!
Won't swallow snake oil hypocrisy!
    Fraud! Mendacity!

This is the revving up of antithesis reality
Vaccinating hate mongers,
This is the antithesis reality & we ain't no foggy mirage
We're slamming your politics of de-civilization
We're the antithesis reality here to reinvent resistance
And to risk revolution
NOT risk lives of tender beings in time of plague

We're coming out of our little boxes
of hope and fear,
to a city near you, a town, a crossroads
We're turning down the static
Voting against capital's extraction of all from all!
We're masked & mouthing the take down

Voting against ugly abusive language,
We are the Antithesis Reality –
    We like to fall in love with whomever
    we want & dance
    in contrapuntal rhythm
We are the Antithesis reality
Voting against reification of land—
    of living earth, peoples, organisms, of water, and air
Voting against borders, drones, cages & carceral torture
Voting against the military-nocturnal-
  techno-surveillance-complex,
    in which power pools, congeals, deadens…
O bare life!   Nothing left to hide! Humanity, keep faith
Come, reanimate the world
O tentacular Nation we're working overtime
This is the antithesis reality & we are here and rising
Power gathers on the flipside of the mobster's cheap penny

Vote against brutality! Xenophobia!
We cheer the proliferation of differences!
Because we are the antithesis reality & we are
entangled in the beautiful rhizome of differences
We're the spooky attraction at a distance growing closer

We are here to reanimate beauty and wisdom!
We intend the possibility of art,

    for transformation & innovation!
We intend to get it revving now

This is the antithesis reality
We earth our charge here,
Extract arrows of broken-hearted Amerika
We'll metamorphosize this techno-thanato-por-
no-punked-out empire
    To the inmost shimmering fabric of the one thousand things of this world!
Don't lose your Mind!

We are the antithesis of reality & we approve this message.

– Anne Waldman

*

From *Beat Roots*

Where was the alchemy in 1961? Where was dear Freddie Herko in 1962 before he walked out the window. And the unguents and libations of velvet life and stammer and conquest and wow. How many arms can one woman have to keep a world afloat? And make babies? This bird—my dove—flies backwards and in all 10 directions of space.

Laboratories and ruminations of the goddess di Prima inhabit The Albert Hotel. One: a brew of herbal elixirs, good for circulation of the blood. Two: the mind of the poet that warms to John Dee because he was a seer. Three: if you could mix sulphur and mercury you would be the perfect bi-sexual. Four: get on stage and act out a scream to dare the elements of invocation. Five: revolution. Six: the rotundity and science of light and cool. Seven: a place in the country preferably underground. Eight: live outside the system, and forever. Nine: barter on the side. Ten: the upside-down fool, welcome him.

I wrote some things down for the future to bank upon, to say the blue. My cards said "obviate", my swords said "rule," my cards said "a sun in your center," my cards said "heartbreak." I started out to walk early in New York–cool, collected–dawn, her Tarot on my mind.

In the language of night revolution

sometimes they kill a loon
who dances like a mad-woman

a picture of desire and fear

newspaper clippings sparse
believe recovery is possible

a blanket fog of waking-sleep
the underworld plunders our means

self-preservation purples
as perfect poems write dreams

language eradicates disease

a new version of old time
revolution not seen on screens
bears witness:

*the only war is
the war against the imagination*

when iris bloom in cities
butterflies turn

toothless dreamers refusing to
see reality: the world may not rise
in this lifetime, but we must try.

– *amy bobeda*

Thank you for being *my bread even after you are gone.*

Amy is an artist from the Jack Kerouac School and founder of Wisdom Body Collective. Her work can be read in *Denver Quarterly, Entropy,* and elsewhere.

There are no words to express my gratitude for *Loba,* and every little glint of my childhood San Francisco preserved in Diane's poetry.

Revolutionary Letter 2021

"to preserve the element of unknown places"–Aldo Leopold

1.
Dear Regenerative Agriculture,
Come our way
All the extra carbon could be taken care of....
in a Degrowth Utopia
Concern that we are just "procedural"?
Know your soil.

2.
Just so you know:
Diane di Prima had full body-spirit of outrage
She was transmitting grounded-ness
Although she studied angelicity
& systems of dialectic art
She was a shield & she was sanctuary

She knew the *skandhas*
Never a hall of mirrors
She opened the field
Justice for all—an ecology of practice & mind

3.
Know sunset, sunrise
Crimson hues of dawn
Moonset, moonrise
How you waited
Know their tongues
What they speak to you
What the thunder said:

Do you want blood to
   come out of me?

Chaos of storm, of fire

Learn lessons of sorrow
Tithe time

Come with your punctuation
Your dharma vow

Be ready to evacuate
Enough for 10 days survival
Keep simple
Have a place to stay
Read The Invisible Committee
Achille Mbembe
The Zapatista Reader
Full Body Burden
The Akashic Records
Sunken Suns.

4.
Who stands in the sun
who was meant
for these firestorms?
    (Loba)

Ask this every day.

Create a shrine of intention
    As she did every day.

– Anne Waldman

Anne Waldman has been an active member of the "Outrider" experimental poetry community, a culture she has helped create and nurture for over four decades as writer, editor, teacher, performer, magpie scholar, infra-structure curator, and cultural/political activist.

One of the founders and directors of The Poetry Project at St. Mark's Church In-the-Bowery, working there for twelve years. She also co-founded with Allen Ginsberg and Diane di Prima the celebrated Jack Kerouac School of Disembodied Poetics at Naropa University, the first Buddhist inspired University in the Western Hemisphere, in 1974.

Revolutionary Letter

Revolution: *return your rage to the earth,*
ancestors whisper as a man, trained in the arts
of inflicting his rage *on* the earth, but fighting
against it—a beautiful distinction—
touches my violated skin.

                    Revolution: when the body cycles, spills
                        rage at the touch of hunter, driller,
                          capitalist scum, stinking mold
                        on the heart of matter, circling
                      wildly we cannot feel movement
                          without a point of reference.

Revolution: what do you give in re-turn?
In completion of a cycle, the cosmos shift
to a new age. Aquarius children dreaming up
old ways to die. This is not new, baby.

                          Revolution: mutiny of language
                          when language fails to describe
                              a history of white
                        bodies slaughtering other,
                  slaughtering queerness, within
                          our soil, polluted
                            our souls in loop
                  holes of burying genocide(s).

Revolution: *you can have what you ask for,
ask for everything.*
Ask to go home
to our mother-place:

Make America Mother Again.
MAMA, remember when everything was
basic human decency? Remember
when home was sanctuary
of health & equity?

    Me neither.

MAMA, I ask
for the first womb,
that dark chasm
(chaos), that next revolt
where hope lives outside
the lines.

                                Revolution: love is here, you
                                                  are love
                          despite the failed attempts
                                        to kill us all
                              this revolution always
                                              rages on.

                                – *Shawnie Hamer*

Shawnie Hamer was born in the heat & dust of Bakersfield, CA. Her first book, *the stove is off at home* (Spuyten Duyvil, 2018) is an experimental art & poetry book curated through a communal exorcism. Hamer is the founder of collective.aporia, an international arts collective featuring online creative workshops & *apo-press. She proudly received her MFA from the Jack Kerouac School of Disembodied Poetics at Naropa University where she was able to encounter the most inspiring group of artists she's ever met–including Diane, whose voice echoes in Hamer's ears whenever she needs the courage to disturb and disrupt.

Revolutionary Letter: Decreation

out of the dark a revolution, a turning, a light
conceived through acts of decreation–

i am unthinking myself, undoing myself
through my body's fine inculcated fabrics
i am only flesh and vacant, reconstructing
"ultimate truth" world notions disintegrate
into nothingness; in the eye of the void
i see the shimmering light of a soul

breaching a placid wave of breath
floating atop the aftershock of thoughts
unthought; we are not that style,
that food, that waste, that version
of convenient sustainability,
that year's model; we are not
that rhetoric, that law, that history

we are turning, turning, turning
the pages of history
and scribing its unwritten verses
in a language we must learn

– C. M. Chady

C. M. Chady's work spans genres, including poetry, fiction, nonfiction, and image. She is a proud graduate of the Jack Kerouac School of Disembodied Poetics, founder of *Tiny Spoon*, an experimental bite-sized literary magazine, and member of Wisdom Body Collective. Diane di Prima's work is an inspiration and calling for the unity and activism possible within poetics and life, inseparable from one another.

Revolutionary Letter:
This Never Before Owned Red

The tongue does not taste itself
Lightning is not loud
I was a human made by my world, wondering
how do we survive
humanity?
While we were being hopeful, bathing
our faces in the King's luminosity, they
were out on the horizon shoveling shit
into oceans. While they
were feeding cupcakes to home-
grown terrorists, handing IEDS out in home-
towns, we were thinking

fly where?

The future has a funny shape
We keep caressing it with our minds
Where will the dust
of gone animals settle? The crumbs of
human action? Hindsight gave out
fur & wings
but when he landed on us
he'd run out of gifts.
So, we got
these tufts
of hair,
no pinions.
What is the rehearsal?
In the forest, the ghosts ate the fruit
and tried to fool us with pits
Dupont Exxon Chevron
Do we stay in the clearing and let them shine
on our reality with their shredding
light?

We unbound
We broke

other animals
down in our bodies
while other things broke down in us
What I want to say is
Proctor & Gamble Dow Union Carbide American Chemistry
   Council
put your fucking money down
and walk into the clearing, you
will not
ever
crush us

but I cried when a bodiless voice said
this civic sentence: *Ladies
and Gentlemen, please welcome our Vice President, and out
walked a woman* — That this thing
withheld so long should feel like a gift?

"What is the sacred opportunity inside this pain?" says Selah.
How do I teach my daughter to bend without breaking? I
   asked.
"I'm trying to get to the point
but I don't know what the point is," my mother offered.
My friends, there is no bridge from here
to Alpha Centauri
there is no bridge
from anywhere on earth there
IMHO, your wild, kind, entangled light
can get me there.

Don't let them colonize your imagination. You
Sometimes put your cell phone down. You
Sometimes put your money down. You
Sometimes put your schooled words away. You
let your colors wilder. You
caress your mother, your
daughter, your
neighbor, your
oak
tree, your
moss, your

child, even
your fish.

These are the actions of words.

– Eleni Sikélianòs

I took a Keats-Shelley class with Diane in the summer of 1989. I wasn't much of a scholar (I was a high school dropout Naropa had found a place for), but I was a reader, and I was an adventurer. Classes took place under the big tent out on the lawn. There was Diane passionately scolding us about our reading habits. "You want to write two hours a day? You've gotta read for four!" That stuck with me more than anything — the fieriness of her conviction. Later, I moved to San Francisco and was reading H.D. on my own; Julia Connor gave me Diane's number and said, *call her*. So I did, and she spent hours talking me through hermetic definitions in *Trilogy*. These gifts we can't account for. Remember having dinner with her, Anne Waldman, and their editor in NY, and how she was *interested* in what I had to say, leaning forward. Remember inviting her to read (with Renée Gladman) at the Poetry Project, and I had to go get her in a cab (a luxury then) because she was afraid of the lightning or the thunder or both. I later lost, somewhere in Denver, the copy of *Trilogy* with all the notes I'd made. Tragic. But I have that more resonant thing Diane offered me: a fiery love of H.D's poem ever lodged in my soul.

Eleni Sikélianòs was born and grew up in California, and has lived in New York, Paris, Athens, Colorado, and now, Providence. A graduate of the Jack Kerouac School of Disembodied Poetics, she is the author of nine books of poetry, most recently *What I Knew* (Nightboat, 2019), and two hybrid memoirs (*The Book of Jon*, City Lights and *You Animal Machine*, Coffee House Press). Her work has been widely translated, and she has been the happy recipient of many awards, including the National Endowment for the Arts, a Fulbright, and the National Poetry Series. She has taught poetry in public schools, homeless shelters, and prisons, and collaborated with musicians, filmmakers, and visual artists. As a translator, she has worked on texts by Jacques Roubaud and Mohamed Leftah, among others. Since 1998, she has been on guest faculty for the Naropa Summer Writing Program, and she now teaches Literary Arts at Brown University.

I Am Alive

Society says "Lose your mind and die to be free"
The god in me says "knowledge is not free but pay attention"
Know the price for living if truly we are dying to live
Do it because you are alive

Yes, I am alive
My life I have
Born as an African
I know I can like Nas

From the street corner with the badge of honour
Gloominess becomes a monument of progress
Autographed by kingmaker and they all kissed the black ring
Night sky is a poet of lightness

The black season of men in greatness
'Pac told me about the rose that grew from concrete
So strong
Hold on
Stand tall and say

I can, I will, I must because I am alive.

Like the portrait of revolution "Lift your fist"
Patrice Lumumba, rest in peace
Let's move like movement
You are the element
We are the future
You better get the picture
Respect nature and reflect culture
Owl knows the language of silence more like making wisdom your gatekeeper
As you defeat your enemy by the power of love just like the heart of Martin Luther the king
Knowledge is king
Flap your wings

Fly
Fly
Fly so high and kiss the blue sky.

– Thickcode

My first attraction to Diane di Prima was how she was nurtured by her grandfather through the practical truth of activism. I read about how she edited *The Floating Beer* with one of my favourite black poets Amiri Baraka. I tried to look for her book *Revolutionary Letters* in Nigeria and I was fortunate to read some of the pages on the internet. She is the definition of leadership.

Tunde 'Thickcode' Dike was the only African that participated in Wroclaw Mail Art Project 2010 "MailUsArt" in Poland alongside 177 mail artists across the globe. He contributed to *No Vacancy* an anthology to support a local homeless in St Louis, Missouri. His poem was featured in a book titled *Unbreakable* written by William Fredrick Cooper, which was nominated for Best Fiction on the 10th African-American Literary. Thickcode currently resides in Nigeria, West Africa.

I Who Am Neither

OM TARA TU TARE TURE SOHA

i.m. Diane di Prima

All souls singing in the bardo
All demon sounds around the etherized fountain
All romances lived out in city gardens and on hidden avenues
All speaking silences that inhabit our own night dense as mist
All rotating calls of guardians above and within us
All stateless peoples without papers who use their rage
   against the state to propel them further into their lives
All one-armed soldiers standing against the future soldiers
   of today
All glass views of towered confinement
All beatic animals stalking in their cautious prowl
All encasing wisdom, all protectors of the teachings, all
   lineage holders
All polyphonic sounds of ecstasy and exasperation
All limitless seeing in mesas and desert hills
All hidden groves of forest that let men sleep
All children wandering the streets of night unshaken and afraid

The wish fulfilling gem is inside the body,
All transient forms of being carry their original light
I harvest my own heart, birth my own child
Mother, you had me, but I didn't have you
Who will come home to cook us supper?
Who will remember to put out the fire?
Who will remain when everyone who's loved is gone?
How do I take this empty seat next to the ether fountain?
Continuing on in this shape, in this movement, searching
But remaining very still

– Mitch Manning
Boston Public Garden
10/26/2020

"Last month I had a dream where Diane and I were reading the Heart Sutra out of a book in an apartment overlooking San Francisco Bay. There was a party. Someone spilled a beer. I quickly tried to clean the beer off the book. Diane looked at me and said, "So what? There's beer on the Heart Sutra. So what?"

Mitch Manning is the author of *city of water* (Arrowsmith, 2019). He's taught poetry in central China and his poems have been read in Basra, Southern Iraq as part of the Boston to Basra Project. He teaches English and Labor Studies. Poems and interviews published in *Battery Journal, The Doris, BOOG City, Let The Bucket Down, CONSEQUENCE, Sundial, Hollow, GAFF* and more.

it'a come (for Diane di Prima)

I met you at the
Dumping Columbus reading
I don't remember the year
2,000-and-something
City Lights bookstore
Italian poets defying
our immigrant ancestors
who thought Columbus was
the ticket to assimilation
our chance to melt in the pot
a mistake for sure
in my copy of
Revolutionary Letters
you wrote
"just under the scorched earth
just under the skin of the old
it'a come
and soon"
I thought of you
the night his statue came
Humpty Dumpty
tumbling down at Coit Tower
we sang "Avanti Popolo"
and "Bella Ciao"
revolutionary Italian songs
no king's horses in sight
did you know that
October 12 is now
Indigenous People's Day
in 130 cities and 14 states
it'a come
Diane
it'a come
but not soon enough

– Tommi Avicolli Mecca

Tommi Avicolli Mecca is a southern Italian queer writer whose work has appeared in magazines, anthologies and newspapers since the late 60s. He met Diane di Prima through the Dumping Columbus readings of the late 90s and early part of this century, which he helped organize. He is co-editor of *Avanti Popolo: Italian-American Writers Sail Beyond Columbus,* which includes Diane's poem "Whose Day Is It Anyway?" Born and raised in working-class South Philly, he lives in San Francisco where he reads regularly at open mics and works at the Housing Rights Committee, a tenants rights organization.

Revolutionary Letter 2021
(January 13, 1989 and January 13, 2021)

I'm keeping Gil on this list,
who knows about the panther gods,
and Anne, who knows how to
invoke them,
Jenn R who makes light
out of dark
with the help of Alpha Cine.

Of the other stars,
include Jane whose porch
bears mule deer
and Orion,
and my brother's friend
Steve John of the
Haudenosaunee Nation.

And then there's you
in the kitchen
on Laguna Street where
Harvey said you cried
over a broken milk bottle
–of course you did–
you were a mom
counting quarters for my
cab fare back to Bernal Heights.

– *Lisa Jarnot*

I found my way to *Revolutionary Letters* circa 1986, age 19, Buffalo, New York. In January of 1989 I was on my way to San Francisco to see the artist Jess Collins. My friend Harvey Brown asked me to take a book to Diane. The book was *Algonquin Legends of New England* by Charles G. Leland. Harvey had apparently borrowed it in the 1970s and I suspect that he was using me as a go-between to heal an old rift. Diane was delighted to see it again and I was delighted to meet her. She said "Come to Naropa!" Instead I ended up moving to San Francisco and living a block away from her at 251 Rose Street at the bottom of the Haight.

Lisa Jarnot is the author of several books of poetry including *A Princess Magic Presto Spell* from Flood Editions 2019. She lives in Jackson Heights, Queens with her daughter and four cats.

My black-haired Cherokee Indian Princess

Great-great-Grandmother,
Chased my blond, blue-eyed
great-great-Grandfather around the house
with a cast iron frying pan.

She was a warpath.
He climbed a tree in the backyard,
He came down after she came down,
having learned a thing about squaw-tipped rage.

He grew right through astonishment into love,
woven like honeysuckle, tight,
into a water-proof container.
She was fiery, but amenable to bedding,
and cooked a right good cornbread.
That kind of love hands down well,
laid back, ironic, true-hearted.

Why she liked him, other than his bringing
back the biggest buck,
had something to do with his arms.
Watching him from the kitchen stoop,
quivering when she heard the axe strike oak,
she never got enough of that
braided leather encircled waist.

She bore ten, lost none before they were grown.
The boys by age fourteen left home,
Girls were eighteen,
she brooked no child-marriage.

That was another thing which made that big man
worth the aggravation,
he would not trade girls.
He carried things for women,
especially young, sleek, black-haired women.

They worked hard and slept well
through changing times.

The photo shows them hand in hand
on chairs in the front yard
near the crepe myrtle tree
in afternoon sunbeams.

Looking the very picture
of contentment, notwithstanding,
she had hurled kindling
at him the night before. He ducked.

When she crept into bed hours later,
he rolled over on his back,
held out his arm, she cuddled in.
He noticed she fell asleep within minutes.

– Sharlyn Page

These are some thoughts that come to mind about this richly powerful poet. Thank you for the opportunity to share them. I am in the process of getting ready to publish my own works and find that such leaders as Diane di Prima, have paved the way for me and so many women who strive for knowledge and wisdom, and voice.

Sometimes the invisible grapevine, or network of minds linked by culture, imparts a meaning to a young life. This is what happened to me when I was very young, and very isolated. My older sister went to university and experienced the beginning of a consciousness shift in freedom. I speak of the freedom of being a woman, a girl who grows into her own power. It was 1970. The voices that rose in that university of the fields in Florida were surely diverse and creative. Yet really new voices, like the voice of Diane di Prima, were not something I heard then. These years later when technology has enabled greater access to works, I turned to Diane di Parma with the recognition that the personal journey my sister and I had taken, was shared, invisibly, with this creative spirit.

Diane di Prima researched the deep past, read mysterious writings, found insight that was far from the interest of the mainstream. These ancient perspectives helped her carve a way to individual freedom. That is something I respect. It is something my sister, who died so young, respected.

In this sense, though I am younger than this poet, we share an historical legacy. di Prima spoke for all young women who felt a sea-change in perspective, looked deeper at life and its possibilities and grew wiser for this. This change grew to be a part of the early Feminist movement.

Wisdom starts with the very young, and nurtured, grows to be the very life of the old.

I wish I had enjoyed the opportunity to meet and share with Diane di Prima. She raised five children, wrote verse with deep psychological insight, and lived her life using her powerful intellect and voice. As a mother to four children, I find kinship in the courage such women represent. I have turned a long life into a search for truth and beauty, and try to put to paper some of what I have learned. These women leaders in their time, like di Prima, enlarge possibility, break rules, and stay true to themselves, as do all prophets and seers worthy of the name. She sought the timeless truths and made them ring loud again in her work.

Revolutionary Letter

'everything is free now'
you said in a poem once
& I laughed at you

Fifth night of insurrection, May 30 2020
written in a looted notebook
w/ looted ink from a looted pen

For those who take what they want
For those who want everything . . .

*

Quiet the two hours before sun,
car whips through empty streets
birds chirp & wind shakes the
leaves, distant sirens, cool air,
ALL cops defeated tonight

Stealing, together, unashamed & loud
breaking in with crowbars, hammers,
trash cans & forklifts, public busses
even, people's own cars smashing
straight into storefronts

Strong & gentle movements of bodies, arms
prying, hands held out to help others over
jagged glass, entire stores emptied
into patient waiting cars, drivers polite,
focused, fast . . .

Tonight alarms RESOUND across america!

Each careful decision, flow
-state of destruction, call it
effortless choreography
of crime

& this is happening
EVERYWHERE people
removing objects of their price
& purpose, giddy sidewalk profusion
breaking glass becoming sand, street
to desert &

more
open space

*

O' if all that capital has taken
could ever be taken back

Not that "justice" or revenge, call it
taking what we want
taking more than what we ever imagined
wanting
taking what we need
taking more than we need
taking what we don't need,
but want
taking what we want to give to others

Not that there isn't OMNI
-PRESENT beauty, already, like a bathroom
full of steam, sometimes you see it
swirling in the air

Not that water isn't life, or that
one could eat money, or Gucci,
not a binary of good & evil, but
STEALING IS GOOD

So call it
positivity
destitution

A Tribute to Diane di Prima   43

direct action
alchemy
WHATEVER . . .
the Zapatistas call it rebellious dignity
call it dignified shopping
call it rage, sorrow, pragmatism
call it proper reaction to murder
call it destruction
call it creation
call it fuck it all
call it heaven on earth
call it joy remaking the world
call it peace

Not that "peace" of Police:
strong armed masquerade
hiding the very body of death,
nor the "peace" of Property:
shiny in your face like you
aren't worthy,
no, but listen, quietly,
really
to PEACE
it means to LIVE
in abundance, never learn lack, not be
hunted, caged, denied PLEASURE,
comfort, luxury, labels, soap, bread,
INFINITE nail polish, to be
loved, saturated, sleeping
soundly on the softest bedding

Not that one could HAVE
any THING as beautiful
as a little voice singing,
or the sun shining
on a face, in the eyes,
over buildings
or mountains o' mountains of
things

*

& later, months later
when all is silent & it snows
for only a minute in a day
of sorting & choosing
of packing up a home

Balanced atop a full garbage bag,
a long-bodied blue dinosaur
stands upon the surface of a bead
framed mirror, becoming
reflective, frozen lake

Accidental sculpture
of surrealist grandeur,
destined for salvation, meaning
destined for a stranger, meaning
I hope one day a mother

Strolling Goodwill, slips the
elongated blue creature into her large
purse & walks out the store, tip
of the tail poking out,
barely visible

– May June

May June is a poet from Chicago who believes in magic and the power of the people.

Rasp of the Revolutionary

Like a sea of stumbling light, the bone needs a scratch,
the bone itself is in needing, in heat,
moaning earnestly like a cat, fossils
crooning under layers of Earth, oil in sharp
plastic too is moaning, singing a scraped throat
song as loudly as the femur of my own allotted body.

Flesh seeks a scratch of its own making, damage,
itch in the iris roots simultaneously calling, *itch.*
The rose quartz is cold and embroidered in
the petals of her clitoris; the sea quivers, then births
while absorbing gallons of carbon from ships.

Mother-aching is an adjective for injustices such as this.

Every being with cells knows every being with cells.

Desire scratched out with a cold knife in an Aspen belly,
fingernails of soft leather from cowhide
hit the sapphire needling of my own breasts
under a magnifying glass at the public clinic,
my stepmother's insurance covers my thighs,
is itching like the ruptured union of celestial bodies,
and the galaxy splatter, too itches.

Solar flares are a reactionary transfer,
cleansing the energy and archetype out of our
collection of bodies, and piles of anything but bodies
in the body sense of bodiness.

Diane, my land, my blue, sacred sky:

There is a tongue of glass that speaks like a ship,
a nipple is another shelf, an altar
for all our potential gods.

If you thread the machine
correctly, there is a woman, delightfully.

If you forget the thread, there is a shell
where a woman used to be, in mourning.

She is there, stradling hallways of debris. She is there,
ready to begin, again, again. To cut it all off with dull
scissor blades, this life hanging unjustly like hair
all around her. To venture more closely into unknowing.

If you get there, please, will you visit me again?

*– Stephanie Michele
2021*

Diane di Prima's words are their own everlasting lineage, are deeply current. Will remain current until no longer as current as now. Until root-level societal change. Until maybe never.

In my backpack last fall, my reprinted copy of *Revolutionary Letters* held space between teabags, frigid notes, random crayons, my bus pass. I carried Diane di Prima all over the city. We want to honor Diane di Prima, revolutionary sister in our ecological, educational lineage, mother of poets, persistent inspiration, community guide, goddess oracle starling, land in which we can nest. We want to honor Diane because her language has forever changed us.

Stephanie Michele is a multidisciplinary performance artist, writer and human being. She currently resides in Denver, CO, lovingly between mountain thumb and city teeth. She holds an MFA in Creative Writing from Naropa University. She is proudly a part of The Wisdom Body Collective & *Tiny Spoon Literary Magazine*. Find her on the internet.

Revolutionary Letter #1 [B]

I have realized that the stakes are not myself and I have
 that privilege.
I have realized that the stakes are many other lives and that
 is privilege.
I have realized I will be okay
unless I put my body in the way
put my body on the line
put my privilege in the way, say,
"this is my white body, this is my white-skinned body, here,
 my tongue,
and here I stay."

Here I've stayed, I have realized, behind the screen, and I
 have that privilege.
But I have realized that the stakes are not myself
unless I put what I have in the way
put my voice in the way
put my voice in the fray
and say,
"this is my white body, this is their body, this is our body,
 here, our hands, here,
and here, stay."

I have realized
many lives fray
like the edges of a rope
undoing, unmaking,
falling from the tree.

I have realized,
and frayed,
and hoped,
and fallen, too,

like a tern shot, on the wing,
like a forsaken partner,
like a grief inherited.

– Robert Eric Shoemaker

While I was a graduate student at Naropa University in fall of 2016, my small cohort of creative writing peers was hit by the seemingly impossible election of a sexist, racist, bigoted fascist-pretender. It blindsided us. From inside our bubble, where everything was ostensibly Buddhist and aimed towards stability and harmony, this result seemed unthinkable. Of course, since that time, we have all learned much about what is thinkable in this country founded on systemic oppression and slaughter. We must learn to be mindful of what history likes to leave out. Living in Louisville, Kentucky over the past year has further taught me the value of self-awareness, especially in terms of privilege and race. The Breonna Taylor movement and the connected movements around the country have proven that, though we are quarantined from one another, we can move forward and stand up. In this time, the hope of Diane di Prima's Revolution given in her *Letters* has stuck with me. What can writers do against the tide when we stand up and recite poetry together and link arms against hatred? Diane led the way, and whether we can even see the end of the road of change, we know it is there because of visions like hers.

Robert Eric Shoemaker is a poet-playwright, translator, and theatre artist. Eric holds an MFA in Creative Writing & Poetics from Naropa University, where he founded activist periodical *BEATS*. He is now a Comparative Humanities PhD student at the University of Louisville. His work has been seen with *Signs and Society, Asymptote, Jacket2, Entropy, Gender Forum, Exchanges, Columbia Journal, Bombay Gin,* and others. Eric has released two books, *We Knew No Mortality* (2018) and *30 Days Dry* (2015) with one on the way, *Ca' Venezia*. Follow Eric's work at reshoemaker.com.

***

The people often eat standing up in the street or walking from this place to that, falling asleep leaning on a cracked glass bus shelter only to be poked awake by police, only to discover that they have been graffitied over, their poofy coat reading in brilliant red 'my dear,' the full graffiti reading, 'My dear, if it is not a city, it is a prison. If it has a prison, it is a prison. Not a city.'

The people never stop working, hauling around all these strange instruments; flutes, seismographs, cast-iron saxophones, oscilloscopes, fugue bugles, contact microphones, squeeze boxes, high-end multimeters, finger pianos, low-end enhancers, scrawled out bits of poetical incantation from ancient manuscripts to address this or that impasse...

The neighborhood horn sections curl off together in mournful twirls, curl off away from themselves in a rough-hewn yet always spot-on unison, the conditions of communication providing them with a redundancy in which they can vibrate.

In the city of our story, you put a sound to an object and the way it responds tells you something about its shape. Every object from the empire state building to a cheese danish has a resonance, a frequency that if you make it, shakes it to its core. This is what the people are searching for, this is what all that research is after.

Searching for some ever-changing artifact of ugly beauty, radiant, absorbent, containing within it the possibility of all questions and answers, a handbook made up of real hands, for the people are looking principally for how to live.

When there is no moon save an eggplant-colored shadow, cardboard umbrellas, streetlight cheekbones, bullet-rain running down the people's arms, people's legs mercilessly, they feel around, blindfolded and without gloves, in the subterranean lairs of fanatics and cranks.

When there is a damp wool sweater drying on the clickty-clack, hissing radiator, the people sneak onto the roof and train in gymnastics as fireworks shoot up from the scarlet street, exploding, burning their hair into hot new styles.

When the state pumps drugs into the people's deindustrialized neighborhoods to prevent any kind of collective empowerment, to promote rot and death, shoveling cash to mineral extraction regimes overseas with one hand and slapping the cuffs on domestically with the other, the people hire chromed-out, snow-white, Lincoln Continental, stretch limousines for fifteen minutes, just to make an entrance.

The people don't follow the news, don't vote, no respect for the landlord, no respect for the business owners, at best ambivalent with regards to any kind of job they have, and much more often outright contemptuous, the young feeling similarly toward school assignments. If they come across the newspaper they use it to sit on a wet bench, stuff it into their coats as insulation, or cut out the pictures to incorporate them into some socio-political collage, for the press is just a tool to manage the expectations of the masses.

No one has ever been interested in what is the most likely thing to happen, but in what HAS to happen, no one has ever been willing to foreclose their analysis of any one situation at the moral. This has been a fiction crop-dusted across the city from on-high and the people just hobnob in penthouses posing as mute poets taking advantage of the refreshment spread.

There are people with parents that have money who want to change the world. These people say you shouldn't help anyone unless you can help everyone, and it's bad to help everyone because then you are helping people who don't need it, then you are helping people that don't really deserve it. These people are like the city's bridges and roads, they take a toll, they are genocidal dividers, they only serve to cause more traffic, producing for the sake of increasing the capacity to produce.

When everything you own is on a sidewalk, it's rather easy for the people of the city to see. They just have to walk down the street. The people are all really existential detectives, all seeking to uncover and map the specific social structure to which they must conform, regardless of what they think, eating only bruised fruit, nervous breakdown legumes, thousands of pounds of cheese, sampling every slice of pizza from the Bronx to Brighton Beach and back again, removing their shoes and hurling them into the cogs of the machine, continuing the journey on bare feet.

The people recite each other's words, wear each other's clothes, eat each other's food, raise each other's kids with absolutely no concern toward what 'the larger cultural conversation' thinks of what they are doing. Mostly because 'the larger cultural conversation' is fucked and has been that way since the advent of agriculture. There is no belief in geniuses among the people and the people never wanted to be individuals, they wanted to work together. The cops produce the individual, the people produce communism.

– Peter Belly

Peter Belly is a worker living in rural new york, working as a printer, stealing time to write and read.

a few words on what *Revolutionary Letters* and Diane mean to me:

I've always thought of *Revolutionary Letters* as one of those books that if the whole history of poetry was destroyed and we just had that one, we would be okay. Like we could build it back. Wouldn't need any more reminding of what it was all about.

I first fell in love with her voice from recordings of her reading when she was very young that I came across on a Giorno Poetry Systems record, "The Dial-a-Poem Poets" I think it was, mid-seventies. This was without even realizing the scope of the project or what she was saying. Just the sound of her voice really did it for me. I was charged by it.

So yeah, Diane always really turned me on and made me happy to be alive and made me feel like I was right all along and that I can't back down and that I have to understand my responsibilities and she gave me a whole, down-to-earth cosmology that made it all make sense together.

Living but Dead Humans

Armed clenched, and forcefully too
Signs of our displeasures over tearfilled events
And showing our strength to say NO
When resolved for the truth to uphold

And the prima facie of our struggle
As in strength and sweat, to show
So, let our arms raised to voice out NO
To corrupt and oppressive rulers
For we have nothing now to lose

Than our long tie to the rope of silly submission
And our vulnerability to fear, and falsehold
Nothing that freedom comes at a cost
Of the river flow of blood and salty sweat
Notwithstanding let the revolution flow too
And wash away fears for a glorious new dawn

For we cannot continue in this perpetual
State of living but dead humans on the streets

– Obinna Chilekezi

I am a Nigerian born poet and my works have appeared in journals and anthologies. My published works are *Songs of a Stranger at the Smiling Coast, My Son Chikeziri died too* and *Calligrammes*.

I came across the works of Diane di Prima from the Poetry Foundation and one of the description of her works in the Foundation's website that touched me most was that her "poetry mixes stream-of-consciousness with attention to form." It will be difficult having such politically conscious poet as Diane. May her soul rest in peace.

Religion Hiding in The Bush

Bad dad force to fail culture
Call in the crone
An edge work sketchiness
Next to godliness lineage
Third mind devotion
I imagine what morning is

    -a new age softer than you and I

Investigate religion humanity archetype
Cartwheel future: this is not the white bourgeois'
questionable creatures

When a crone looks you in the eye, you look back
When a crone goes to story, you listen
Listen these witches are working into the mystery

Listen these crones are turning into stars
Hunting justice. Haunting halls.

Until the day the mayfly flag, the flags were prayer and
prayer is certainly still one thing worth taking up a flagpole.

The crone down the way is slapping clay to beasts and
bodies of love. The crone on the salt's drying juniper to
burn. The juniper's a crone their own.

Lumen: crone

Lux: crone

Needlepoint: crone

Piercing rays: crone

A Tribute to Diane di Prima

One crone's a bushwhack wire and bristle brush under the chin.

What symbol would embody the universe?

whisker?

watch?

If you're an old queer crone, the nursing homes on the access range'll closet you right back up to keep the peace.

If you're a snarl tooth, they'll forget you got a word to talk.

> listen listen.

> crone. god. monster.
> crone. god. monster.

Oh who do you think waters these flowers?

"If my notebook's not run out of batteries yet, the notebook's still for writing."

Regards,
Crone

> And now let us speak of the Dark Goddess Crone.

>> Oh the night of men has been a tower.
>> A ship sunken sea.

> A Yaga would eat 'em warm-blooded.
> A Hera would transmorfification.
> Would deep sink the sea.
> While palm red pomegranate in hand.

Crone Council Check-Point: a silver and you're in.

Tests of treaty: star-bound and for the cause

Crone Points: a swamp witch story, a crow, a wild-turn story, sewing skills, snarf and snow, suns (one crone a sun), belly dance and pin point, push with a wooden spoon, and pat pat, a poem (one crone a poem), a crooked hop, a goodness-my, a rotten tooth, a sly, baked goods (one crone a baked good), a sneer, a caw, a bottle for the moon, a smokescreen (one crone a mystique), garlic, a night

– Ana Anu

Ana Anu (she/they) is a poet and multi-media artist. Their work, centering eco-feminist poetics, has materialized in two books of poetry, *Noon* (2017, thisisfeministart press) and *Mona Mona Mona* (2019, thisisfeministart press) and through large public discourse performances and installations internationally. Anu is an MFA candidate at Naropa University where she is co-teaching in the Interdisciplinary Studies program. Anu is a current U.S. Policy Partner Fellow with the U.S Partnership for Education in Sustainable Development, applying their 10+ years in Environmental Consulting to influence Sustainability Policy as an educator and arts organizer. Anu organizes BIPOC scholarships on behalf of the International Council of Thirteen Indigenous Grandmothers as well as artist residencies at This Is Feminist Art.

Much gratitude and my deepest respect to di Prima for modeling revolutionary realness, for digging up the tresses of goddess traditions, for embodying the bodhisattva witch, and for serving as one of our most beloved crones in council. May she rest in power and haunt in justice.

I ask myself the questions to walk the labyrinth city in silence with the air as a canvas

realizing the subject was a border and I have no destination except arrival. I return to the question exhausted of myself. This is what I know and how I don't. I am a dissipate, the enemy of something and you are together it is human the breath is good and the war was bad, very bad. Everything else is mostly just talking to myself. I get along fine when the temperature is right.

I carry a piece of paper in my pocket when I go for walks. By the time I get to the water nothing has been written on. It is still your letter as I walk alone to the water immerse the edge of the paper in so slight and dip ink from my veins. You could write, here, the poem says. You should right here the mind says. What would you do here? What do you want? I want the poem without the loss. I want to save the attachment. To share a moment without giving yourself away is to misunderstand how time works. We can make the most of time we cannot make more time. I can turn this time into a piece of paper send it to the souls make them days with it but my moment is gone all I am left with is the glory. It will make for a good story. Hey do you remember the time you wrote that poem spot in the moment I think I still have it in my pocket. Oh we were so vain then though it beats the pain we are in now trying to remember the impossible and getting further away from it. We got away with it. We got away with our language memories objects and bodies. We got away and nobody cared. They didn't come looking. We sent them self addressed letters. They didn't write back. They've never written at all. It is not what those moments are for. You can keep the blood in your pen you never know when it will come in handy. Play with your hands while your hands wait for something to play with. You can play with me tonight. I'll be by the water, writing.

– Matt Clifford

Matt Clifford is a poet and musician from Denver, CO.

In every step of my poetic path, Diane di Prima has showed up. Because Diane di Prima showed up. She showed up on the page as present and powerful as her more heralded contemporaries; she showed up off the page, in community, in conversation, teaching, serving. Because that's what a poet does–shows up and does the work. Diane demonstrated that in the alignment of her values, action and art. And she kept doing it. She did it her whole life, with humility and fun. For Diane di Prima's life was the life of a poet, and for the path she has opened and allowed me to follow, the lineage she has set, I will always be thankful and do my goddamndest to honor.

Revolutionary Letter: Small Stirrings

Revolution as in
rotation
the next turning
in a predicted arc
perhaps we set ourselves up

Sitting under the shadow
of a yesterday
that was once called night

Years ago, I stood on the seaside coast
outside Shanghai
saw the world's first sunrise
from the vantage point
of tomorrow

Letter as in
an envelope sealed shut
closed carrier of meaning
a commenting on the passage
of time or a catalyst
for slowing it down
like the tide's slow rhythm
returning glass to sand

I dreamed I gave birth to a moon
that on second glance
was an oak tree
its branches and roots reaching
in all directions, a globe

I hear they are trying to move the forest north
to clothe the land where
it will turn to grassland
in the changes to come
I picture figures moving trees one by one
each carries a version of the self
turned upside down

dendrites reaching as roots
waiting to be reunited with dark earth
of yesterday

My body twists in worry
as I look out my window
the grass bare and yellowing
as I try and bleed
like the sky tries to break into snow

Is the lake ice cracking because it is melting
or because the water froze
on a day with wind

A discordant sound
like the rattle of unfallen leaves
in a midwinter wind

And at times the sun
looks like the moon
behind thin snow clouds
its edges only visible
in obscuration
until it returns
obscuring the view

― *Emily Trenholm*

Emily Trenholm is a multi-genre writer and teacher from Minneapolis, Minnesota. She is currently pursuing an MFA from the Jack Kerouac School and is a member of Wisdom Body Collective. She admires Diane's work for its call towards deeper revolutions.

Revolutionary Letter: Dianaesque

Stop and breathe, people. November, December 2020, January 2021 will be the strangest political and psychic weather we've encountered in a long, long time.

Hunker down, button down, stay loose, stay centered, stay light and graceful.

Nonchalance, brio, bravura and *sprezzatura* are our cloaks, our ponchos, our opera capes.

Get enough good food, get enough sleep. Be grateful if you are privileged, tenured, have a big chunk of your paycheck excised for Cadillac health insurance that's repeatedly saved your life. Yet always feel that what you enjoy in life is also deserved by all others among us.

To fund health care for all only means taking money only from big Bezos and the 1%, from the brontosaurus Baluchitherium budgets of the swollen unnecessary military overseas, at home in bases, and enshrined as local police.

Appreciate how fragile our system of urban, inter-urban circulation is when your car goes dead, there's not public transportation, and even though you could afford taxicabs but don't even need those because you're teaching online from your house, let your heart fill with awareness of those who can't easily get to where they've got to go.

Realize that after age 60, certainly 65, with emergency urgency at 70, everything tangible, fungible, material thing that you own diminishes your quality of life as much as it enhances it. How many books can you give away?

Agree the system is flawed, we need self-governing institutions outside of it. Then also roll up your damn sleeves and support the Bernie Sanders, the AOC and Squad Sisters, and Black Lives Matter patriots who push and kick its windows and doors open, march in and expand its famously promised opportunities to all.

Offer the guarded kindness to frightened conservatives you would a troubled delinquent child, but sneer at open-carry Gun Queers as the sexual minority they are, a predatory one that needs strict rules and enforced privacy (not display on public streets or in statehouses).

Let nothing, not even your beloved, interfere with your recording of your dreams first thing in the morning. Savor your reveries of brilliant ideas over your big cup of coffee. Gently butterfly-net all epiphanies that flutter to your grasp during the waking hours of the day.

And subvert Them, the Spectacle, the Man, their reign of neurotic terror by smiling. Please, and thank you.

– Mike Mosher
Bay City, Michigan, USA
November 10, 2020

I knew Diane was an important poet when I saw her read in San Francisco. I was in my late twenties, and she was about fifty. I had seen her daughter Mimi delivering a stirring rap at a political demonstration in the Mission a few weeks before, and now when I saw Diane, what struck me about her poetry was how *motherly* it was. Whatever she read at that venue had the kind of sound, caring, button-up-your-overcoat advice that warms the *Revolutionary Letters*. As a young teen, the pounding White Panther Party rhetoric of John Sinclair was in the Michigan air (and MC5 free Sunday rock concerts!), so I was used to more macho revolutionary stances.

Old Sedan (Revolutionary Letter 2020)

Moving by sound—
had it been birdsong, or a penny,
had it been elected to serve us,
had it figured as a kind of childhood
in which wherever we stand is never stable,
and nowhere the vigor we want to drink
which we can down even while we are shouting
about the train of time stopping here
right in front of us,
get on,

someone tells us what to do—
even the well-intentioned people
who speak, who listen,
can't keep it all straight sometimes,
and it's so strange
how these times parse among us the hard bread,
forcing us to put it in our mouths
as if that would hush what needs to be said,
at least
by those of us who have lived
and we, what is "we" anyway
I ask you

where should we focus our listening when every sound
(not of love, not of future) is a shout,
and our neighbors all look alike in their jackets
the colors of smoke and asphalt,
and someone wears a scarf the red of an old sedan
peeling away so hard half the tire tread remains,
and who's that calling for help somewhere among our shoulders
in a voice I might have recognized six months ago
before we folded around ourselves
and covered our mouths—

how do we enter the language of the raw,
what is thunder broken into 300 million pieces
where no one can take a full breath

because of what thrusts from our throats out of control
as if there ever was a best kind of control,
a kind control,
if only things were kind here outdoors on the street
where it's needed
the privacy of a heartbeat now out in public
but I don't want them to stop,
don't stop,
hearts, don't stop

– Jayne Marek

During the weeks I spent in Paul Nelson's recent Poetics as Cosmology / "Spontaneous Composition" course, Diane di Prima passed away, so Paul focused some class attention on her "Rant" and *Revolutionary Letters*. My piece directly resulted from my renewed reading of my original copy of *Revolutionary Letters*, which still contains the energy and urgency as when it first appeared—as many of us have noticed. Previously, I have published several poetry books and chapbooks, including *In and Out of Rough Water* and *The Tree Surgeon Dreams of Bowling*. I won the Bill Holm Witness poetry award and have been nominated for Best of the Net and Pushcart Prizes. My poems and art photos appear in *Bombay Gin, Spillway, One, Chestnut Review, Silk Road, Eclectica, Grub Street, Calyx, Cortland Review, Folio, About Place, Stonecoast Review, Slipstream, Inlandia, Women's Studies Quarterly, Sin Fronteras / Writers Without Borders, Notre Dame Review, Gulf Stream, Watershed Review,* and elsewhere.

Revolutionary Letter for Pear Tree

Perhaps if I write this letter, hope follows. Two weeks ago my grandmother had asked me to come into the backyard to pick up a dead animal with a shovel. She had said that she could not find herself to stare at it, witness it in its death. Rotting.

Before each meal, she prays and gives thanks for the food she has in front of her. She says Amen and eats her meal in silence. Mi abuelo tells me a story of an unattended fire underneath a mesquite tree. A tarp that sustains itself as a home for him and his family. Working the land. Changing the land. Para un mundo exacto, extracto. Si había una revolución era una de oro. A golden vanity. Beating telephone wires. The systems that fail. His one year old brother, a brother I did not know dies of starvation and sickness. Working the land. Changing the land.

I had forgotten about the idea of growth through a spreading sheet glass. Skin opening wound. Yesterday, in the middle of a white man's voice I lost hearing, sight. How will things end with your bloodline? A war inside the womb. Curtain revealing a promise, a mistake. ¿Cómo se acabarán la sangre de tu linaje? I do not think of those consequences of the past anymore. I count the number of birds on a tree. Academia shoving itself down my throat. And within all these words I ask where is the Revolution? Where is Justice?

This week I write questions to interview the poet Ebony Stewart. In one poem she writes, *"Us poets whose duty is to write about the times write because we don't know when we too will become extinct."* The wiping out of a material thing. A poet breathing lungs into words. I ask her in response, *extinction within this country, within the world, is recurring and in most cases through violence. How as poets can we prevent extinction from happening? Or remove moments of violence?*

    Layla sends me a recipe for a pear tart. I tell her of a dream I had two nights ago where I planted two pear trees. Both growing. Learning. Lo que va cambiar, va a cambiar, Mama says.

    And again, and again we arrive.

    A sweet pear tree that even bears fruit in the cold winter.

– *Diana Lizette Rodriguez*
February 15, 2021

To follow an impulse such as Diane di Prima is a removal of the flaccid tendencies a female body poet is placed to exist in. The Revolutionary Letters are instances where one can hear the echoing words di Prima once said, "Well, nobody's done it quite this way before but fuck it, that's what I'm doing, I'm going to risk it." To risk it, to run into the uncertain placements of which living truly as oneself is a revolving action to the endless tending to living history.

Diana Lizette Rodriguez is a Mexican-American artist from San Antonio, Texas. Rodriguez is a graduate from Naropa University studying underneath the Jack Kerouac School of Disembodied Poetics and Visual Arts department. Rodriguez as an experimental artist finds and places herself steadily in the relationship of text and image. Rodriguez enjoys fragments, disorientation, and waking up early in the morning before anyone else wakes.

WEFT 3

I have almost no ideals when it comes to beauty.

A repetition of images makes me think I've alighted on beauty, but by the time I claim it, it's just a stain.

Greater minds than mine expand the circular wave of circumstance.

I heap myself against a ridge then fold over.

I think I believe in something, but each day my strong feelings grow weaker.

It is like this very bright sun in December degrades my faith in the fibers of connection.

My daughter has so much confidence in what clothing can produce.

She dresses in what's at hand and becomes the exact thing she wanted.

She has almost no memories.

So little has happened to her.

A person, even a very small person, can wend a way through all this clutter.

She wends a way by melding with it.

In five years, a person can master everyday life.

This is what I mean by permanence.

Our tactics may be flawed, but they make our presence nonnegotiable.

What is the thing we want ourselves to be?

I want to do my work in the morning.

I write a poem, and the poem is like a window.

I open the window and the insects enter.

All the insects clamoring for blood.

I will return to the skirt lying on the table.

I'll unfold the skirt with my rough hand and smooth it.

I will turn toward the skirt this time and really describe it.

But it's too late.

My poem has made me sad.

My sadness is wrapped around my finger and the perfect body of my child.

– J'Lyn Chapman

J'Lyn Chapman serves as an Assistant Professor in the Jack Kerouac School at Naropa University. Her book *Beastlife* was published by Calamari Archive in 2016. Her most recent work is *To Limn / Lying In*, published by PANK Books in 2020. She has also published the chapbooks *A Thing of Shreds and Patches* (Essay Press, 2016) and *The Form Our Curiosity Takes* (Essay Press, 2015), both of which can be found online.

I admire di Prima's *Revolutionary Letters,* and I feel miles distant from them, I'll be honest. But I wish where I worked was named after her, and my revolution is a slow process of seeing the ways I've failed and am trying harder.

Revolutionary Letter

To the young revolutionaries:
Don't think yourselves invincible. Your bodies
if they live to age will break
and ache and stiffen with frustration
even as they spring into acts of resistance on
demand and there will always
be more battles to fight - don't
spend too much strength, taking
extra time on the short
story when you're really constructing a
novel approach to the next
phase of evolution.

To the old revolutionaries:
Don't think yourselves wise. That's for others
to decide behind your back, maybe long
after you've passed from this plane and
your name only exists on the lips
of the young, who can't remember if it was you
who said that thing you said, as they repeat it
incorrectly – the truth you pass on
is what remains of your voice as your words
become memes if you are lucky and religion
if you are not.

To the middle-aged revolutionaries who
can't wrap our heads around how
this title applies to us now when we
thought we'd be long gone at
the hand of the state or
the one attached to our own wrist:
Don't stop. Our beating hearts are
needed even when they're bleeding
from the stab wounds of the
ones we once called comrades and
the pain will not subside but it will be
transformed into power.

– Emily Yates

Emily Yates is a constantly-changing brain in a slowly-deteriorating meat suit who identifies as a writer most of the time and an overthinker all the time, and who can usually be found puttering around in her fairy cave, setting unpopular opinions to catchy tunes. Her first encounter with Diane di Prima's work was with "Buddhist New Year Song," which inspired her to embrace her inner alien, and reminded her that even broken mirrors still reflect.

Dear Kin,

This is a revolutionary letter because it is uncensored.
There's so much traffic that all the signals
cross and fragment.
I hope I make contact.
Letters are a contact sport, after all.
See also: sex and theatre.
Coming to you from dysmorphic dysphoria land: my head.

Tears well up in my chest, a storm goes underground. It's mostly dust up top. Big sky. O' Beaver Moon, dreamin' shadows. There's no getting dizzy in switchbacks when you are Mountain. What is void if not something to enter, pass through? Nothing is forever.
We bleed together.

Inch by inch we weave the web. Uterus is a sensitive keeper of time.
Here's to healthy self-soothing, banishment of myopia!

Potential unrealized is wishful thinking.
I had the key in my pocket the whole time I thought I was locked.
What if there were not anger habits to get locked up in? No fear habits. No greed, dull senses, nor numb heads papered with numb flesh.
Would they still say we need prisons and prisoners, then?

What if the good fight is the just one you have with yourself when you're wrestling
with will power and positive change?
There was a trapdoor in the dream, something beyond
root cellar with its canned peaches.

Speaking of roots,
it takes a lot of energy to break ground in the dark.
Let us give thanks to the mighty microbes and fancy fungi feeding all follicular gestation. Cellular restoration is happening in this body even in moments of pain.
Change and Compost are the true god and heaven.

We all get there, eventually.
Good Orderly Direction is something my Mom called god.

Snake Medicine states that magic is nothing more than a change in consciousness.
When the moon went dark in Scorpio I thought about killing myself; became the intrauterine shame, labored with those contradiction contractions, integrated and gave birth to someone freer and saner

Transmutation
Transposed into language by conversation. Such memories are muscular.

This may be the year of the metal rat, but it is the time of the Phoenix.
Breathe.
Your existence is sustenance
is anarchy
is lovely.

– *Ada McCartney*
November 2020

Nothing is as important in the world as doing your work.

Ada McCartney is a poet studying with the Jack Kerouac School at Naropa University, a member of Wisdom Body Collective, and a teacher. When she first read *Loba*, it broke her open to the magnitude of a woman's poetry. With deep gratitude and love for this work.

Find her at www.aamccartney.com

October 26, 2020

Diane died yesterday
she instructs me still
remembering
thou we first met at Bard in '64
I watched her kids for her
we truly met at Huey Newton's funeral in '89
we were two white women
dressed to the nines
out of respect
mentor, friend
walk past clamoring chores to finally sit down and write
Diane wrote in the Poetry Deal pass a sink full of dirty
dishes to go to poetry

pass the clamoring mind
to my Haibun Journal after Diane
teaching me still

voice happens
all round me
my pen and paper
capture bits of it

my body
needle
my life
thread it
slowly begin
to make my day

it's hard to find the eye
I can't see it
without assistance
easy to become distracted
every moment
every turn of the mind
is crowded
messages about Diane

every word is inadequate
even suspect

years ago Diane and Sheppard gave me a pale salmon
colored lotus candle
today I lit it for Diane
today I also picked up The Ones I Used to Laugh With –
Diane's Haibun Journal
it's miraculous
thank you
thou you have died
you teach me still

laid aside
much is laid aside
the chocolate bar wrapper
                            with the beautiful John Donne
                            love poem
extreme dark
Diane instructs me
bright flame melts the lotus into her

– Timotha Doane

I first met Diane di Prima at Bard College in 1964. She had been invited to read there by Robert Kelly. She was macrobiotic at the time. I watched her kids while she went shopping. I really met Diane, and we became friends, in Oakland, California in 1989 at Huey Newton's funeral. Diane became my teacher and mentor in life and poetry. I attended her many, over years, poetry/writing workshops and programs. Our friendship was grounded by Vajrayana Buddhism, poetry, and a desire for restorative justice.

Timotha was born in the midst of World War II in Corpus Christi, TX on March 22, 1944. Her father, first lieutenant in the Coast Guard, was patrolling the Gulf of Mexico looking for German war ships.

Timotha, chodpa, gate player, has pilgrimaged in Tibet, Nepal, India, and Bhutan following the footsteps of Machig Lapdron, an 11C female Buddha/saint. She has climbed to 14.8 thousand feet to sit in ancient, sacred, buttery caves with her sangha.

She is a life-long torchbearer and priest on Hekate's path.
She practices Vajrayana Buddhism and western magic traditions every day.

In the past, she has worked in solidarity with the African People's Socialist Party. She is now in solidarity with the Black Lives Matter movement and the movement to abolish prison and the death penalty. She is studying whiteness and white supremacy and working with her sangha in SAWS, (Severing Attachment to White, Supremacy).

She is queer.

These are the myths, identity markers, signposts on the trail of an authentic life. You will not see them.

She has published the broadside *Taboo* and a chapbook, *Bahamian Journal*.
Timotha lives in San Francisco with her husband and the sustaining love of friends and siblings.

i do not believe in death

i do not believe in death
but still i cried / tears visit like angels
soundscapes of your life
the way you came in / space you filled
language studied you
you're not in the stars
that's too obvious
maybe in the rim of your favorite mug
or the bristles of the paint brush
you last touched
experiencing the same things you loved
from a different perspective
will bring you cannoli & espresso soon
but i don't believe in death / i can't
don't make enough sense
i believe in the soul
in transformation & change
i believe in the essence of mindfulness
(poets are masters of this kind of thing)
reframing pain / turning everything into beauty
seeing you live / being close to you
just proves i'm right
death is not real &
life is a reflection of the soul
you were magic   still are
brought life to its knees
fangs for eyes
as you drew blood from flowers
and turned concrete to gold
the way you conquered ink   and became the page
spoiling us with your genius   leaving

a bit of poetry on every closed eyelid
isn't the most natural response to beauty
to savor it in the mind

– chani di prima

"i do not believe in death" was written the days following my grandmother's passing and is what i read at her memorial with the immediate family.

chani di prima is born & raised in bay area and is the eldest granddaughter to diane di prima; a self-published author, poet, philosopher, and spiritual teacher.

Layout design by C. M. Chady

Title font: ITC Bookman Std, 15 pt
Body font: Bookman Old Syle, 11 pt
Bio and notes: Minion Pro, 12 pt

Cover Design by amy bobeda
Original image from *Memoirs of a Beatnik* by Diane di Prima

More Revolutionary Letters was conceived, midwifed, and birthed by the women of Wisdom Body Collective: Amy Bobeda, C. M. Chady, Ada McCartney, Stephanie Michele, Emily Trenholm, and Chloe Tsolakoglou.

This project was community created and funded through our Kickstarter campaign. A portion of books printed will be donated to Naropa University's Jack Kerouac School to support the Harry Smith Print Shop.

Wisdom Body Collective is a process-oriented collective. We seek knowledge of the body, sensations and memories it gathers as it navigates the world. We are an artist collective open to those called to embody and create through the female spirit. We teach, create, and learn from each other while helping nourish creativity.

Founded by a group of writers from the Jack Kerouac School of Disembodied Poetics, WBC aims to cultivate a more original form of expression, through the body, and through the sacred feminine.

Discover more at WisdomBodyCollective.com.

Inspired by what you've just read?

Send your own revolutionary letter to
WisdomBodyCollective@gmail.com
to be considered for Volume 2 of
More Revolutionary Letters

WISDOM BODY
an artist's collective